Stratford-upon-Avon
in old picture postcards volume 2

by Patricia McFarland M.A.

European Library ZALTBOMMEL/THE NETHERLANDS

GB ISBN 90 288 6283 8

© 1996 European Library – Zaltbommel/The Netherlands

Introduction

The twentieth century is drawing to a close and its beginning is recalled only by a very few very elderly people and by postcards and pictures and writings reflecting life before two world wars brought unimagined changes in the life of our town. This second volume of 'Stratford-upon-Avon in old picture postcards' recalls the first half of this century and the events which pre-occupied Stratfordians in those former days. The first half of the twentieth century in Stratford certainly seems to have belonged to the Flower family, principally Archibald (later Sir Archibald) Flower, whose life revolved around the Borough Council, the Memorial Theatre and the Shakespeare Birthplace Trust, and the family brewery. Other members of the family, Sarah, Edgar, Spencer, Arthur, and later Fordham and Dennis, were also busy with improvements and developments in the town and concern for the townspeople. And there were other notable families.

Stratford-upon-Avon was intensely loyal to its sovereign and royal visits were popular, royal occasions extravagantly celebrated, and royal mourning carefully observed. It was also an artistic town, in the widest sense. We loved to decorate the streets, to dress up, process about the town, produce dramatic and musical events both amateur and professional. Local people have always been called upon by the professional company performing in the Memorial Theatre, when extras were needed.

Local residents still don costumes and join the annual Shakespeare Birthday procession, still present plays and operatic offerings, and still patronize the professional theatres now developed from the former Shakespeare Memorial Theatre.

There are, sadly perhaps, fewer local businesses, but fifty years ago the tradesmen of Stratford still formed the backbone of the town and the Borough Council and were patrons of the many flourishing sports clubs.

The year 1996 is one of commemoration in Stratford-upon-Avon. In 1196 the Bishop of Worcester granted borough status to Stratford and the same year Richard I authorized the first market for the town. It is also the 500th anniversary of the death of Sir Hugh Clopton, who became Lord Mayor of London, built the bridge over the Avon and endowed the Guild of the Holy Cross, whose legacies still enrich the town. Four hundred years ago the arms of the Shakespeare family were granted and Shakespeare's only son Hamnet died. It is two hundred and fifty years since the first recorded performance of 'Othello'. So it is fitting for Stratford to reflect on its twentieth century history too, with images of some of those moments to take into the next century.

The Garrick Jubilee in September 1769, celebrating William

Shakespeare probably marked the beginning of the tourist pilgrimage to Stratford. Since then millions of visitors have been drawn to the town which, besides being the birthplace of William Shakespeare, has become famous simply for being famous. The domestic life of our town goes on despite the congestion of vehicles and pavements and riverside and Stratford hopes that those who come will find something of the real life and history with which we live.

This volume would not have been possible without the facilities of the Shakespeare Birthplace Trust Records Office and its complete archive of the Stratford-upon-Avon Herald, from whose pages I have quoted extensively. The Records Office Senior Archivist, Dr. Robert Bearman, his assistant Mairi Macdonald, and Eileen Alberti, were endlessly and patiently helpful and interested. All the photographs are from the Records Office collection, with the exception of No. 40 (Golf Club opening) for which I am indebted to the Stratford Golf Club.

1   Flowers on Shakespeare's tomb

The Shakespeare Birthday Celebrations, 23 April 1900, came only a month after the relief of Ladysmith in the midst of the Boer War. That news had been received with riotous celebrations which turned, in Stratford, into riots in which several alleged pro-Boer (anti-war) tradesmen had their windows smashed and premises damaged over a three-day period. The Shakespeare Festival was limited that year to one week, but events were reported in detail in the Stratford Herald, which described 'perhaps the most striking of the events recorded... being the decorating of the poet's tomb, a pretty custom which becomes more popular with every year'. This year the Vicar, the Reverend George Arbuthnot, devised the ceremonial at which the Mayor and Corporation and the Shakespeare Club processed to the church and presented floral tributes to be received by the clergy and laid on the grave, followed then by members of the congregation with their flowers. 'Long after the service was concluded the church was thronged with people anxious to view the decorated grave.'

2   Theatre-goers in Chapel Lane

In 1901 Queen Victoria died in the 64th year of her reign. The Soldiers of the Queen became the Soldiers of the King in the still raging war in South Africa. Perhaps it was the sense of history in the air, but for the first time since the Shakespeare Festival at the Memorial Theatre began in 1879 the Historical Cycle, 'the Week of Kings', was presented in sequence. W.B. Yeats visiting Stratford that spring wrote an elegiac description of the effect of the history plays, 'played in the right order with all the links that bind play to play unbroken... the theatre moved me as it has never done before'. The town flocked to these performances. Yeats wrote: 'Inside I had to be content with an extra chair for I am unexpected and there is not an empty seat.' During the two-week Festival Frank Benson's company presented twelve Shakespeare plays, the week of history and a week of comedy.

3   Edward VII Coronation procession

Plans for the Coronation of Edward VII on 26 June had had to be postponed when the king became ill, but in every town and village they came to fruition on 9 August 1902. In Stratford there were street parties, the illumination of the riverbanks and boats, a decorated bicycle parade, 'Old English Sports' (flat races, obstacle races, tug-of-war, comic football etc.). The Borough Council in specially convened assembly moved a resolution composed of Shakespearean quotations to be sent to Their Majesties, including 'Peace be to England, What danger or what sorrow can befall thee, So long as Edward is thy constant friend'. Councillors then processed to Holy Trinity for the special Coronation office, adapted for use throughout the empire. After the service the Council processed to the site of the new free library in Henley Street.

4 Laying the library foundation stone

A week before the Coronation the Mayor, Councillor A.D. Flower, received from the Earl Marshal, the Duke of Norfolk, the following message: 'I am commanded to invite you to the Coronation, August 9th. Please telegraph whether you can accept the invitation. You must wear robes and chain: if no robes, uniform or court dress with chain.' His Worship replied: 'Much regret that local mayoral duties prevent me from accepting invitation for August 9th.' (Did all those invited get only one week's notice?) The laying of the new library foundation stone added to the Stratford Coronation celebrations. The Mayoress received the silver trowel from Edgar Flower, her father-in-law, who said 'he presumed he had been invited (to take part) partly because he had always taken such an interest in the adjoining institution (the Technical College) and partly because the ground on which they stood happened to be his'.

He then dedicated the land to the Free Library. Edgar Flower died the following year.

5   Mop Day 1905

'One Mop,' the Herald observed, 'differs very little from another... the principal characteristic being of course the roasting in the public streets of oxen and pigs.' This 1905 scene in the High Street outside the Garrick Inn (before its Tudor frontage was restored) was repeated outside other public houes. A 1902 report said: 'Eight oxen were impaled and roasted whole in the customary fashion and several carcases of pigs were subjected to the same fate... Stratford cooks know exactly the heat required and so perfect is the process that not a particle of the carcase is wasted.' The annual Mop Fair on 12 October had long since ceased to be the hiring fair from which the name derived and had become an event given over to enjoyment, a street fair with 'elaborate entertainment paraphernalia... for the thousands who, on amusement bent, set aside the sterner duties of life to devote themselves unreservedly to the mirth-giving facilities of fair time'.

6 Fairies from Midsummer Night's Dream

The local newspaper review of A Midsummer Night's Dream which closed the 1906 Festival season at the Memorial Theatre recorded that 'there were sprites, elves and fairies without number'. Not only without number but also apparently without names. However, on 12 June Sir Benjamin Stone, manufacturer, traveller and President of the National Photographic Record Association, and Lady Stone entertained the fifty or so children of Stratford who had taken part in the Festival performances. Tea was spread on tables at the back of the theatre and afterwards the children danced again the dances from Midsummer Night's Dream to warm applause. Sir Benjamin recorded the happy occasion and also inaugurated the Nine Men's Morris court in the theatre garden, in the presence of the Mayor and Mayoress and other invited guests.

7   Valentine and Freeman, 20 and 21 Bridge Street

This location in the town centre is a good illustration of the evolution of Stratford shops. When the century opened Mr. A.E. Parkhouse was an established draper and outfitter in No. 20 Bridge Street on the left of the picture. In No. 21 Valentine and Freeman, milliners and costumiers, had replaced Mrs. S. Wells, a draper for many years. By 1906 Valentine and Freeman had absorbed Mr. Parkhouse's business and expanded to occupy both premises, but whether wisdom or economics prevailed, No. 20 was sold to Algernon Whitcombe, an art dealer and later Borough Councillor, who opened his Shakespeare Gallery there before the First World War. Valentine and Freeman continued at No. 21 until 1924 when, after extensive 'tudorizing' it became the National Provincial Bank. Whitcombe's Shakespeare Gallery and Restaurant survived into the 1950s, until it too was taken over by a bank. It is still a bank, but No. 21 is now an ice cream parlour.

8 The Hospital Stall

The Hospital Saturday movement was formed to augment the funds for the local medical charities and in 1907 the Hospital Stall was set out at Market Hall at the top of Bridge Street on 14 September. It was organized by Miss Cottam, the Matron at the Hospital, and Miss Mosely, the Superintendent of the Nursing Home. Fruit, vegetables, flowers, and home produce of all kinds were contributed for sale. There was a donation of dressed poultry from Mr. Gibbin, who had donated the site on which the hospital had been built in 1884. This year a decorated bicycle parade and competition was added to the attractions, the entry fees going to swell the funds. The Town Band contributed their services and volunteer collectors circulated through the town during the day.

9 Marie Corelli's Gondola

After a period in the doldrums, a new Boathouse signalled the revival of the Stratford Boat Club in 1900. Marie Corelli, its patron, had generously donated prize cups in 1900 and a handsome King's Trophy Vase in 1902. She and the club had several differences of opinion, all very publicly aired in the newspapers, as was her custom. But by the time the annual Regatta was revived in June 1905, peace reigned and she presented her King's Trophy Vase to the winners of the open fours race. A 1908 Herald report of the Regatta said: '... a reserved portion of the river was filled with punts and boating craft in which reclined maidens attired in the daintiest of summery garb, while up and down the banks the mere men followed the racing with the keenest interest and in flannels and blazers they made a brave show and were the cynosure of many an admiring feminine eye...' Marie Corelli in her Gondola was an annual attraction at Regattas until 1914, when her gondolier went off to war.

10 Birthday procession in Church Street 1909

Of special interest in the Birthday celebrations of 23 April 1909 was the attendance by the American Ambassador (Hon. Whitelaw Reid) and the Norwegian Minister (His Excellency M.I. Irgens) to unfurl their countries' flags. A reporter said: 'We can foresee a time when most of the countries will be specially represented at this gathering.' Other countries' flags were unfurled by eminent local burgesses, the Mayor (Councillor Priest) unfurling 'the King's flag'. He then led the company along the decorated streets to the Town Hall, where he and the American and the Norwegian, as well as Dr. Sydney Lee of the Birthplace Trustees, spoke of their pleasure in the occasion. The procession then moved along Church Street where the headmaster and boys of the Grammar School took their places at the head and led the long throng with their flowers to the special church service and the presentation of wreaths and bouquets to decorate the poet's grave.

11   Re-opening of Harvard House

Having taken upon herself the protection of Stratford's heritage, Marie Corelli arranged the purchase of 26 High Street by Edward Morris, a wealthy American. It was to be restored to its Tudor glory under her supervision, and because John Harvard's mother, Katharine Rogers, was born there, she intended it to become the home of Americans visiting Stratford. On 6 October 1909, in the presence of the American Ambassador, Whitelaw Reid, the house was formally re-opened, named Harvard House and donated to Harvard University. In her opening remarks Miss Corelli described the details of the purchase saying that the worthy Stratfordians had had a chance to step in to save this locally unvalued house but had missed it. Harvard House had now been rescued for all time. Harvard and America and Stratford had all benefited from this gift to the wider world. Miss Corelli presented the Ambassador with a silver casket containing the massive wrought-iron key to the house.

12   Proclamation of George V

Loyal Stratfordians mourned the death of King Edward VII on 9 May 1910. But the throne of England is never vacant and his son was immediately proclaimed King. In Stratford the Mayor, Alderman Deer, summoned the Council and officers at 8 a.m. that morning and those available processed to Market Cross. A fanfare of trumpets introduced the Mayor who read the proclamation. 'Whereas it has pleased Almighty God to call to His Mercy our late Sovereign Lord King Edward the Seventh of Blessed and Glorious Memory, by whose Decease the Imperial Crown of the United Kingdom of Great Britain and Ireland is solely and rightfully come to the High and Mighty Prince George Frederick Ernest Albert...' At the conclusion of the lengthy proclamation the band played the National Anthem and following three cheers for King George the Mayor's procession returned to the Town Hall to make their corporate speeches and appreciations and to make preparations for the civic funeral observances which followed on 20 May. The rest of the annual spring Festival was abandoned.

The Proclamation of King George V S. on A. May 9th 1910

13 Presenting Frank Benson with the Freedom of the Borough

Frank Benson, a favourite with Stratfordians, had been, with his company, the mainstay of the spring Shakespeare Festival since Charles Flower invited him in 1886 to come to the Memorial Theatre. In 1910 he was preparing to add a summer season. A special Council meeting at 5 p.m. on Monday 25 July was called to carry out a Council resolution of 26 April to confer the Freedom of the Borough on Frank Benson, only the second person to be thus honoured, the first being David Garrick in 1769. The Mayor, Alderman Deer, presented the illuminated citation, in a carved oak casket. The citation read, in part: 'In recognition of the eminent services he has rendered to the borough and to the nation by the single-minded devotion with which he has laboured to awaken throughout the world a more lively and abiding sense of the true value of the works of Shakespeare, our greatest townsman, (and) to hereby admit the said Francis Robert Benson to be a honorary freeman of the borough of Stratford upon Avon.' After the ceremony Mr. and Mrs. Benson were taken round the town in an open carriage, greeted everywhere by flowers, friends and admirers. It was also their wedding anniversary!

14   The Daily Mail plane over Stratford

'An airman has at last been seen in Shakespeare's country,' triumphed the Herald. On Wednesday, 24 July 1912 Stratfordians were thrilled by a succession of wonderful exhibition flights by Mr. M. Salmet in the Daily Mail plane. He flew that morning from Worcester and after circling Pershore and Fladbury landed briefly in Evesham before heading for Stratford. As soon as the plane appeared over Bordon Hill the Stratford crowd already assembled on the Bancroft and the Recreation Ground gave a great cheer. The plane circled and then 'volplaned down in an exceedingly graceful manner' to the Recreation Ground, where Mr. Salmet was warmly welcomed by the Deputy Mayor.

15   The Daily Mail plane on the Recreation Ground

Once on the ground Mr. Salmet was greeted by the official party including the town clerk and the Borough Chamberlain. Frank Benson 'flew down – on foot' from the theatre to offer his congratulations, saying: 'I am an actor on a lower plane. You are in a higher plane.' Before leaving the Recreation Ground the airman expressed his hope that when he came again next year many present would be flying. 'It is so easy,' he said, 'there is no dust, and if you meet an enemy you do not pass by on the other side, but just fly above.' Before departing he gave a 'marvellous exhibition, flying between the trees, diving over people, and skimming the river like a bird'.

16 Opening the new bandstand, 10 May 1913

'A bandstand is, or should be, a necessity in every town that caters for visitors.' At last, declared the Herald, we could claim to possess a bandstand where the Town Band could discourse sweet music. Thanks to the fund-raising efforts of the Band secretary Septimus Usher and the admirable work of the Borough Surveyor, Roden Dixon and the builders Messrs. J. Harris and Sons, we had a structure it was our duty to protect. The Mayoress, Mrs. Ballance, herself an active supporter, opened the gate with a silver key presented by Mr. Rupert Boyden of the Band Committee (seen in the centre). He hoped that 'when music was a little more cultivated in Stratford large crowds of people would enjoy music in the gardens'. This bandstand, set in the Bancroft with the Memorial Theatre in the background, was moved in 1929 to the Recreation Ground, demolished in 1966 and rebuilt and opened in August 1995.

OPENING NEW BANDSTAND STRATFORD-ON-AVON MAY 10 1913 C.T. SERIES No 2

17 The Town Band

It is usually possible with the help of the archives to discover who was present, in what capacity, whenever formal occasions and speeches were reported. So it is noticeable that the Town Band seems to have been made up of nameless musicians. The local news columns would anounce: 'The Town Band will play on the Bancroft on Saturday next.' The proprietors of the Hippodrome gave the proceeds of a concert to the Town Band, several of whose members gave selections in the course of the evening. But who were they? From the annual report of the Band Committee we know who made even the smallest donation and that the bandmaster's name was Hind. That two of the members were named Bradley we learned many years later. Why did no one bother to identify the men for whom the new bandstand was erected?

18   Women's Suffrage Society

The suffragettes were making many headlines in 1913. In June a note in the Herald announced that the National Union of Suffragists' march to London would reach Stratford on 16 July to be met by local suffragists at the bottom of Bridge Street to form a procession to the Fountain where a meeting would be held. The local organizers wished it to be distinctly understood that the pilgrims were not in any way associated nor had they sympathy with the militants who had brought so much mischief on the cause. In the event the meeting was disrupted by a vast crowd booing and jeering and shouting down the speakers. One or two of the 'champions' of the suffragists were badly dealt with by the crowd and the disturbance, said the newspaper, 'does not reflect credit on the town or the residents'. The event was not as benign as our postcard of the gathering by the Fountain shows.

19 Bank Holiday pageant 1913

Frank Benson's influence was seen in the re-introduction of May Day Revels and pageants which were enthusiastically joined by the whole town. In 1913 'this wonderful dreamer' extended this idea to produce a Bank Holiday pageant, and the whole day was spent celebrating with a long costumed procession of floats and tableaux. One subject depicted was the visit of Queen Henrietta Maria in 1643 (during the Civil War) to meet Prince Rupert. In the procession, the Queen 'robed on a noble charger' was preceded by standard bearers and men-at-arms and the banner 'God for Queen Mary'. On each side of the Queen walked three girls with floral garlands, while close behind rode the lady-in-waiting. The day included old English sports on the Recreation Ground and demonstrations of early local industries like basket-weaving and wool-stapling.

20 Warwickshire Yeomanry, spring 1914

The Troop Roll of D Squadron of the Warwickshire Yeomanry, which included Henley-in-Arden, Stratford-on-Avon, Weston-sub-Edge and Salford Priors, was reported to be at full strength as they began their 1914 'encampment' at Warwick Castle, 23 May to 6 June. The Yeomanry Sports on Whit-Monday attracted many trippers and 'a select and fashionable attendance in the enclosure', members of the county gentry being present to watch the many competitions between the Yeomanry and the Royal Warwickshire Regiment. D Squadron won the Section-Jumping, Wrestling on Horseback and the Balaclava Melee, were runners-up in the VC Race and lost the Tug-of-War to C Squadron. D Squadron was reported the strongest in the camp. A month later Archduke Ferdinand was murdered in Sarajevo and in August the Yeomanry went to war.

21   Warwickshire Yeomanry leaving Stratford

'Recruits are needed immediately for the Warwickshire Yeomanry. A reserve regiment is being formed for general service at home and abroad and the terms of enlistment offer a special opportunity for young men who have a knowledge of horsemanship and firearms.' Young men flocked to join up as the war against Germany took over the country. The Herald on 31 July 1914 had said that no mobilization of the British forces had been ordered and reported that 'the interesting suggestion had been made in Berlin that Great Britain, France, Germany and Italy should formulate a plan to "punish" Servia (sic) which would satisfy Austria and to which Servia might submit.' A month later the Warwickshire Yeomanry were leaving town, Stratford furnishing some of the 'best and smartest of its population'.

22   Town Hall Hospital

Ten days after the outbreak of war the Council gave notice that the Town Hall would convert to hospital use if needed. By October refugees from Belgium were pouring into this country and a call went out for accommodation for them. Wounded Belgian soldiers were also in need of care and the local hospital and the improvised hospital at the Town Hall were full. The Hon. Mrs. Hodgson expressed in print her gratitude for the kind help she had received towards equipping and supplying the Town Hall hospital. Lists of donors of money, sup-

plies and promises were all printed and further donations requested. The names of all the Belgian soldiers being treated at the Town Hall were also printed. The Memorial Theatre governors had kindly

made premises available for Belgian refugees and donations of furniture, bedding and household goods were requested by the Mayor, as well as other premises or hospitality for the refugees. No. 2

Guild Street became known during the war as Belgian House.

TOWN HALL

23   Major Bairnsfather and his sons

Major T.H. Bairnsfather of Spa House, Bishopton, late of the Indian Army and a Justice of the Peace, was put in charge of the local recruiting office. He was also in command of the General Duty Reserves (Home Guard). His name was constantly in the Herald, encouraging enlisting, supporting the Mayor at fund-raising events and appealing for recruits with special skills, like shoeing, harness-making and sadlery, for which the standard requirements of height and chest were waived provided the men were in good physical condition. Major Bairnsfather's son Bruce (on the right) became famous for his wartime cartoons, featuring the Tommies, Old Bill, Alf and Bert, and 'The Better 'Ole' ('if you knows a better 'ole go to it') about life in the foxholes of No Man's Land. A bitter poem called 'My Dug-out' which appeared in the Herald of 19 February 1915 was signed only with the initials B.B. and would not likely have pleased the recruiting officer.

24   Mounted troops in Church Street

With mobilization came the urgent need for horses. Requests went out for anyone who had a horse to spare for the war effort to make it available. A cautionary letter to the Herald early in the war, written by Lord Redesdale, warned that taking horses that had not been used to work straight off grass and putting them on to oats before they were fit, would result in unruly or broken beasts. Scarcely a month later the Warwickshire Yeomanry horses at camp in Newbury stampeded through the town causing panic to passers-by and damage to premises and to the beasts themselves, many having to be put down. The pleas for, and shortage of, horses continued throughout the war, though the increase in vehicular transport gradually replaced them.

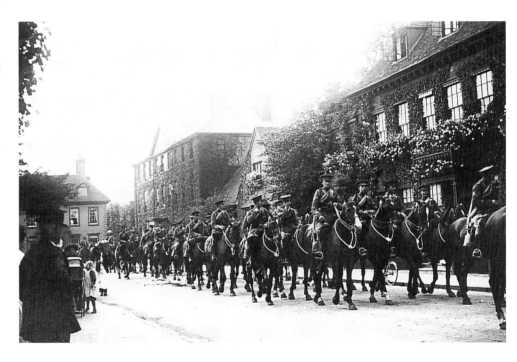

25 Whytegates Voluntary Aid Hospital

In May 1915 the Hon. Mrs. Hodgson announced that the Town Hall hospital would close and would reopen at Whytegates in St. Gregory's Road under the name of the Voluntary Aid Hospital. Mrs. Hodgson, the tireless organizer, was Vice-President of the Stratford Division of the British Red Cross. The Principal Medical Officer of the Red Cross, when he toured the Town Hall hospital, pronounced it a model of its kind. Mrs. Hodgson publicly thanked all those who had helped with time, money and gifts of any kind. She hoped the generosity would continue in the new Voluntary Aid Hospital. Whytegates, under Dr. Earnshaw Hewer, opened as a hospital in a scheme which included the Alcester Road hospital and the new war hospital at Clopton House, the Hodgons' home.

26   Patients at Clopton War Hospital

As recruiting lists lengthened, so did the casualty lists and Stratford hospitals were under great pressure. A typical news item announced that 108 wounded soldiers had arrived, 77 'carrying cases' and 31 'sitting up' patients. They were taken in borrowed ambulances and private cars to Whytegates (thirty of the 'sitting up' cases), fourteen stretcher cases to the local hospital and the rest to Clopton War Hospital. The names of the private car owners were printed and thanks conveyed. Stratford's war efforts were unfailing, with treats for the convalescent servicemen and fund-raising for equipment. Even the Mop included stalls for help for the war effort. The Military Service Bill was passed in January 1916 and War Courts became a regular event in town as magistrates, including Major Bairnsfather, met to hear applications for deferred call-ups or exemptions.

27 Food queue in Wood Street

Serious shortages of food dominated the newspapers. Rationing of sugar began early in the war and at the beginning of 1918 the authorities announced immediate rationing of tea, butter and margarine. There were regular bulletins in the papers from the Food Control Committee. A large notice appeared in early spring urging every man who had a garden or allotment to plant potatoes saying that in 1917 the country had produced 39,000 tons of potatoes, but consumed 125,000 tons. Make the country self-supporting! There was even talk of ploughing up New Place Garden. All strawberries that year were commandeered for jam. Whenever word spread that a scarce product was available, a queue like this one in Wood Street materialized.

28   The Avon in flood
23 april 1918

Shakespeare's Birthday 1918 was a dispirited affair, after nearly four years of war. It was not helped by the great snowstorm two days earlier, which was followed by heavy rains. For nearly 24 hours rain and snow fell making it one of the wettest and bitterest days of the whole winter. On the 23rd the water was still rising and boat owners were having to secure their boats. Frost and snow had already damaged the fruit trees, seriously affecting the coming season's crops. Flags were unfurled that day but no service was held at the church. Canon Melville went to the church to receive what few damp floral offerings were brought to the poet's tomb. No wonder the reports described the birthday celebrations as 'maimed'.

29 Peace luncheon

The war was over but the War Notes continued in the newspapers into 1919. Hospital patients still in the temporary hospitals were entertained; American officers awaited their return home in the comfortable quarters provided by Marie Corelli in Trinity College. There were still food regulations. But by 19 July the country was celebrating the signing of the Peace Treaty and in Stratford the celebrations were wide-ranging. One event was the gathering of ex-service and service men who assembled and paraded to the cricket ground and after speeches of praise and thanksgiving for their brave services, and re-membrances for those who did not come back, they moved off to a spacious marquee embellished with red, white and blue streamers and the shields of 'notabilities' of Stratford of bygone days. A feast of cold beef, mutton and ham, new potatoes, salad, sweets and pastries and beer and lemonade was 'served by a battalion of fair waitresses'.

30 Stratford Technical School Football Team

Peacetime activities returned to local life and rugby, cricket, association football, golf and tennis reports replaced the war news in the weekly papers. Schools, villages, clubs and businesses all fielded teams and leagues were organized. Despite striking miners, terrorism in Ireland, unions organizing everywhere, the sports events took place regularly. In April 1921 '...The Technical School met the Railway Reserves on the Loxley-lane ground on Easter Monday, when the former team won by one goal to nil. The Mayor (Councillor Fox) kicked off. The match was in aid of the Hospital Maintenance Fund, the happy suggestion of the Technical School players, and one in which they are to be commended.' The collection taken on the field was £1.19s.

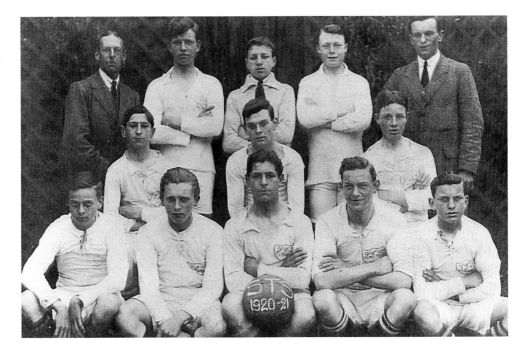

Another favourite peacetime event was back in the calendar with the return of the annual regatta. Saturday, 18 June 1921 was a beautiful day and a whole day's events included swimming displays by men's and women's clubs, as well as competitions, water-polo, and the many rowing events. The local crews held their own and acquitted themselves well, taking into account that they were not seasoned oarsmen. With all the attractions offered by itinerant vendors the atmosphere was almost that of a miniature Mop-day. The area set aside for punts was as well occupied as in pre-war years.

32 After unveiling the War Memorial

In volume I of this series the scene of the unveiling of the War Memorial on 12 February 1922, was one of massed crowds around the high cross draped with the national flag. Without the flag and the crowds the names of the 235 men of Stratford who did not return from the war could be read. The ceremony had been attended by four local clergy, the Mayor and Corporation and members of the Royal British Legion, as well as military and civilian representatives. The Herald commented that it was fitting that the cross was unveiled at Market Cross 'where the footsteps and trafficking of their townspeople may echo about their shrine' and 'not in some quiet garden where only birds and the drone of insects might break the solemn silence'. The 'trafficking' knocked the cross off its plinth in 1927 and after a period in the Bancroft Garden it now indeed rests in the quiet of the Garden of Remembrance in Old Town.

33 Regatta Boat Club picnic 1922

Another Regatta, but less successful than last year's with dull skies, fewer entries and smaller crowds. An unfortunate accident marred the event, caused by a steamer cutting across the path of the Hereford competitors as they were winning their heat in the King's Trophy Challenge. The prow of the Hereford boat was smashed and the crew were unable to row against Stratford in the final. The Stratford Club sportingly withdrew from the race making Hereford the winners. The competitors were all treated to the Boat Club picnic. An extra attraction was the exhi-bition of the self-styled world's champion high diver, one of whose feats included diving 80 ft. into 4½ ft. of water fully dressed and smoking a cigar, and emerging with the cigar still alight.

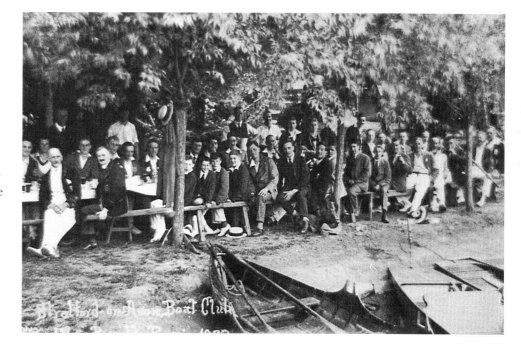

34 Visit of the Prince of Wales on 14 June 1923

Royal visits had been few and far between – 1806, 1830, 1868 and 1897 – so 14 June 1923 was an important day for this very loyal town, and intense and complicated preparations had been made for it. The Town Centre was closed at 3 p.m. and the Mayor received his guest at the borough boundary at 3.45. The band sounded a fanfare of trumpets and played the National Anthem and, as the entourage proceeded up Bridge Street, God Bless the Prince of Wales. At the Town Hall, His Royal Highness inspected the 280 guard of honour of the Royal British Legion before entering to receive an address from the Corporation. Tea was served for 225 guests before the party moved to the Birthplace to be received by Sir Sidney Lee and shown the treasures there, and to sign the visitors' book. All this occupied only fifty minutes, after which the Prince of Wales departed for Birmingham. Messrs. Joseph of the aluminium works presented all the 1,600 school children with collapsible cups, suitably inscribed, as a memento of this special day.

Arrival of H.R.H. The Prince of Wales at the Town Hall Stratford on Avon June 14th 1923

35 Marie Corelli's funeral

Shakespeare's Birthday celebrations in 1924 were already blighted because the official opening of the British Empire Exhibition at Wembley that day prevented many from accepting the invitation to Stratford. The Shakespeare Club luncheon had to be cancelled, but the annual meeting paid tribute to Marie Corelli, who had died that week. Stratford on the day of her funeral, 26 April, closed its shops, drew its blinds and fell silent as their most famous resident was taken from her Mason Croft home to the Parish Church and then to the cemetery. Hundreds of tributes poured in from high and low and even those for whom she had proved a scourge mourned her passing. She was a generous benefactor and patron of many societies, fighting like a tigress for what she believed, attracting controversy but seeing herself, as one writer said 'a winsome, warm-hearted, sunny natured woman'. The heavens wept that day and the town was a duller place thereafter.

One subject dominated the 1925 news. On the last page of the last issue of the Herald in 1924 were descriptions of two proposals for the solution to the relief of the 15th century Clopton Bridge which was, even with its 19th century repairs and modifications, totally inadequate for 20th century traffic. The Ministry of Transport asked the 'famous architect' Sir Reginald Blomfield to inspect the site and report. He didn't like either scheme and proposed his own which the town didn't like. So began a series of proposals and counter-proposals, mostly involving the pedestrianization of the Clopton Bridge and a new bridge just upstream with new roads leading to it. Week after week through that year the newspaper and the Corporation deliberated, with Ministry of Transport advice and many varied drawings and plans. A grant from the Ministry was even offered, but far below the costs. As could have been predicted, because no agreement could be reached about what plan was best and who would pay, the Clopton Bridge remains almost unaltered, and the relief road and bridge were not to be for another sixty years.

STRATFORD-ON-AVON.

Captain Bruce Bairnsfather had become internationally famous. His characters Old Bill, Alf and Bert, and 'The Better 'Ole became a huge stage success and later a film. His popular cartoons of the battlefield were reprinted and sold in thousands. The British Legion naturally adopted his cartoons in their recruiting drives. At a meeting of the County Council of the Legion in May 1925 fund-raising and 'propaganda work' were the main topics, with one member suggesting that Poppy Day should be on 11 November throughout the country. Bairnsfather's career as a playwright and film-maker, featuring his wartime characters and the service life, were a great encouragement to Legion recruiting and kept the Old Soldiers in the public eye long after the cessation of hostilities, and he was still drawing cartoons in 1939 when war came again. He died in 1959.

Whatever else happened in 1926 Stratford's greatest event was the spectacular fire at the Memorial Theatre on Saturday, 6 March. It was not just a local, but a national and even international sensation and the press took the opportunity to air their various views of the theatre. The Daily Telegraph critic wrote: 'No one could honestly maintain that the Memorial Theatre was worthy of its purpose or its site. It was built half a century back when the standard of taste in this country was not high, and it looked like an ogre's castle escaped from some German fairy-tale.' Now that 'fire from heaven' had descended no commentator had a good word for Charles Flower's monument. But undaunted Archibald Flower immediately started a rebuilding fund and the annual Festival went on in April thanks to the local picture house.

39   Sir Whitworth Wallis Memorial

When Whitworth Wallis came to live in Stratford after the First World War he brought a whirlwind of activity and enthusiasm to a wide variety of organizations. As Keeper of the Birmingham Art Gallery since 1885 his monument already stood in that building and its collection. He was an eminent organizer of international exhibitions. In Stratford he re-organized the Memorial Theatre picture gallery, was a trustee of the Birthplace, gave sparkling lectures and after-dinner speeches to everyone from Grammar School prize days to Working Men's Clubs. He was an active clubman and sportsman, played golf, tennis and billiards, was an oarsman, amateur actor and master of make-up and character parts. He was described in his obituary as a man of volcanic energy. In a dark corner of the Parish Church a monumental plaque was unveiled in 1930 to Whitworth Wallis, Kt. J.P., F.S.A. He died on 16 January 1927.

40   Golf Course opening

Although the Stratford Golf Club moved to its Tiddington Road location in 1925, after 27 years at Welcombe Fields, the directors decided to postpone the official opening until the course had settled. Samuel Ryder, a frequent visitor to Stratford from his home in St. Albans, was President of the Club in 1926, the year he presented a gold cup, the now famous Ryder Cup, for competition between American and British professionals. He was invited in 1928 to bring four professionals to play 36 holes of exhibition golf to mark the official opening of the Stratford Club and Sam Ryder was invited to drive the first ball. The day's golf was followed by a gala dinner at the Shakespeare Hotel for Mr. Ryder and the professionals. Archibald Flower, proposing the toast to the guests, described Sam Ryder in theatre terms as 'golf's great impressario'.

41 Opening of the Hospital extension

The Stratford Hospital which had opened in 1884 had gradually, over the years, added to its facilities and was generously patronized by constant fund-raising and gifts. The extension fund begun in 1921 finally provided the means to add new accommodation and facilities for the nurses and the official opening was held on 30 May 1928. Lady Helen Seymour, whose late father-in-law, the Marquis of Hertford, had been President of the Hospital for 25 years, performed the opening. The photograph shows Lady Helen seated with the Mayor and Dr. Latimer Greene standing and the Reverends Frank Hodgson and Canon Melville on the right. The sum of £2,477 of the necessary £3,100 had been raised and the remainder was confidently anticipated from generous residents. Alas, it is all a memory now. The hospital was demolished in 1995.

42 Charter members of Stratford Rotary Club

Monday lunchtime Rotary Club meetings were already established at the Shakespeare Hotel early in 1928. But on 4 June its President Alderman Ballance received the Charter for International Rotary Club number 2776 in the presence of more than twenty of its local members and forty representatives from Midland clubs. The originator of the Rotary movement, Paul Harris, had visited the town that weekend (but was attending luncheon in Birmingham that Monday) and had been conducted round the town by the President and Robert Lunn, the Hon. Secretary. Mr. Harris was especially interested in seeing the portrait of Edwin Booth which American Rotary had presented to the Memorial Theatre. The names of charter members still find echoes in Stratford nearly seventy years later – Flower, Winter, Organ, Rowe, Boyden, Morgan. The Charter was inscribed 25 February and signed by the President and Secretary of Rotary International, and of Rotary International of Great Britain and Ireland.

43　Cutting the first sod – Clopton Estate

With the 'interesting ceremony' of cutting the first sod on the building site of the new housing estate along the Birmingham Road, on 8 March 1929, a start was thereby made towards the building of one hundred houses which, said the Mayor, Councillor Annie Justins, 'would bring comfort and improved conditions to many families'. The houses were described as '76 of three-bedroom, non-parlour type at a cost of £324. per house and 24 two-bedroom, non-parlour type at £296. per house'. The Mayor expressed the hope that 'within twelve months the housing problem in Stratford-on-Avon would be satisfactorily solved'. The main road in the Clopton Estate was named Justins Avenue.

44   Foundation stone laying

Elizabeth Scott's design for the new Memorial Theatre had won the competition in 1928, but the Governors decided in March 1929 that the Birthday Celebrations on 23 April were already heavily programmed. So the laying of the foundation stone for the new theatre was deferred until Thursday, 2 July. That day the full panoply of Freemasonry assembled, headed by the Pro Grand Master of the United Grand Lodge, the Rt. Hon. Lord Ampthill, who performed the ceremony with the assistance of the Assistant Grand Secretary with the trowel and many other officers of the Grand, Provincial and local lodges, bearing the maul, the plans, the standards and the full paraphernalia of a Masonic occasion. Nearly seven hundred Freemasons in full regalia, collars, aprons and gauntlets and many Craft and Royal Arch jewels, joined the Chairman of the Governors (Archibald Flower), the Mayor and Corporation, the architect, the theatre company, and hundreds of towns people. The Herald commented that several of the Masons present had been at the laying of the first foundation stone in 1877.

45   Freeman – Sir Archibald Flower

The 1930 New Year's Honours list included the name of Archibald Flower, recognized with a knighthood for his heroic work in raising money through tireless travel and crusading for the new Memorial Theatre, as well as for the years since the beginning of the century when he assumed responsibility for the Memorial Theatre and the Shakespeare Festivals. At a private investiture on 17 February, at Buckingham Palace, King George V made him Sir Archibald Flower. At a special meeting on 10 March the Borough Council paid its own tribute to their long-serving member by conferring on him the Freedom of the Borough, and presenting him with a model of 'his' new theatre, then under construction on the site of the old one.

The 1930 production of the Amateur Operatic and Dramatic Society was Sir Arthur Sullivan's 'Rose of Persia' with words by Captain Basil Hood, based on an idea borrowed from the Arabian Nights, and performed at the Picture House on 27, 28 and 29 February. The photo shows 38 members of the cast which was directed by Mr. Henry Tossell. The local critic was not kind to the production, although he said there were some particularly good individual performances. However, at the beginning Persia seemed a long way off and Warwickshire much in evidence. The Royal Guard, he said, looked suspiciously like Fred Karno's army. The eastern dances, however, were extremely difficult and were intensively drilled by Sylvia Atkinson. The dancing was good, concluded the critic.

Stratfordians have always loved dressing up and performing and any opportunity is enthusiastically embraced.

47   The Mayor and the schoolchildren

Councillor R.M. Smith was Mayor in 1931 and that year he chose the week of 19 October to entertain the 1,400 schoolchildren in the town. He gave parties for the infants and some of the juniors in their own schools, and the other juniors and the seniors he treated to a film at the Picture House, followed by tea with paper hats and games and entertainment at the Town Hall. Monday, Tuesday and Wednesday three hundred children at a time enjoyed this treat. The film was 'Simba', a film chosen for its educational content, being a record of an expedition in Kenya. The Mayor said that he enjoyed himself more than any of the children, and they thanked him with a present. The town clerk, Robert Lunn, as their spokesman, told of the 'secret society' for collecting a penny from each child, and the gift was a cigar and cigarette box in silver. The Borough Chamberlain had organized the music and skits, and a good time was had by all.

48   Prince of Wales opens the New Theatre

On 23 April 1932, following intense preparation and high excitement in the town, His Royal Highness Edward Prince of Wales arrived at the new Memorial Theatre at 2.15 p.m. to unfurl the Union Jack, the signal for the unfurling of all the other flags of the nations represented. Stepping on to the dais, he then performed the opening ceremony in a speech broadcast not only to those in the Bancroft Gardens, but by relay to America (where so much of the money for the project had been raised). He was then accompanied by the Mayor and Chairman of the Governors of the Theatre (Sir Archibald Flower was both) to the door of the theatre where the architect, Elizabeth Scott, presented him with the key. The performance, before the royal guest, that afternoon, was Henry IV Part 1, with a special preface written by John Masefield, the poet laureate, and read by Lady Keeble. The Birthday luncheon that day had been served to six hundred guests.

49 New Bancroft Promenade

To give the new theatre its proper setting, the Corporation and the Great Western Railway had co-operated in clearing away the collection of buildings on Waterside which had been an undoubted blot on the town's landscape. So it was appropriate that the day before the royal visitor was to arrive the Mayor officiated at the inauguration of the Bancroft Promenade linking Bridgefoot with the theatre. The Mayor said he was old enough to remember when the ground was a great wharf and in 1886 had been dedicated for public gardens and taken over by the town.

The Great Western Railway had helped by letting the town have the ground for a third of its value. The borough engineer then handed the Mayor a pair of scissors, for which he paid a penny, and after cutting the tape he led a procession the full length of the Promenade, where he cut a second tape.

50 Floods in Swan's Nest Lane

'Monday's Great Flood' said the Herald headline following the 1932 Whitsun Bank Holiday. On Sunday night, 15 May there was a torrential downpour and by 9 a.m. Bank Holiday Monday part of the Recreation meadow and the cricket ground were under water, and the riverside path in the Bancroft Gardens was flooded. The Boat Club's large raft broke away and went over the mill weir. Holiday campers in the Warwick Road meadows abandoned their tents. Bishopton and Shottery properties too were flooded and the Birmingham Road premises of N.C. Joseph Ltd. suffered serious damage to stock and materials. Mr. Joseph said the Corporation sewers were too small to cope with even an ordinary rainstorm – a thundering disgrace, he called it. 'We are not an expensive hotel catering for visitors to the Memorial Theatre (so) nothing is done and we do not suppose anything ever will be done.' The Swan's Nest Hotel, though catering for visitors, probably agreed.

51 Crippled children's motor picnic

The first week in July 1933 was hot – too hot to eat, some thought. Nevertheless, on 6 July thirteen generous motor-car owners provided Stratford's crippled children with a substantial picnic including ice cream and fruit and they all set off in convoy at 2 o'clock for a tour of the Cotswolds, through Alderminster and the Fosse Way to Moreton-in-Marsh and Stowe-on-the-Wold, where they stopped at St. Edward's Hall for a stretch and for 'pop and bananas'. Then after a drive through Broadway and Welford they were home tired and happy in the early evening. The outing was organized by Councillor E.P. Ray.

52 First Mayoress's badge

Although the Mayoress had customarily taken a prominent part in civic functions, and often been the Mayor's delegate at many of the more social events, she had never had any insignia to identify her publicly. This circumstance was rectified when on 22 April 1934, at the Town Hall, after the Shakespeare service in the Parish Church, the Mayoress, Mrs. J.H. Rowe, was presented with the new official Mayoress's badge, a small replica of the Mayor's badge on a gold chain, subscribed by the Mayor, Aldermen and Councillors. Alderman Flower, presenting the badge said that having been seven times Mayor he along with almost a dozen former Mayors in that room knew how often the Mayoress represented the Mayor at civic functions. Mrs. Rowe thanked the Council and expressed her great pleasure and honour at being the first Mayoress to wear the symbol of office.

53　The Gower Memorial

On its original site (see No. 6) the Shakespeare Memorial sculpture by Lord Ronald Gower, unveiled in 1888, had created problems. Because of its location in the grounds of the theatre the public had to pay a shilling to view it. It was supposed, said many, to be a gift to the town, not to the theatre and ought to be available free to all. The destruction of the old theatre and the building of the new one offered an opportunity to re-site the monument on public land, by 1932 cleared and landscaped, near the Basin. By spring of 1934 the group of statuary was reassembled with the four Shakespearean characters moved away from their original positions at the base of the monument, opening out the whole effect, but detracting perhaps from their connection with each other and their author.

54 Visit of the Emir of Jordan

Stratford is accustomed to visitors of all sorts and nationalities and most pass through the town without attracting much attention. But the visit of His Highness The Emir Abdullah Ibn Hussein and his entourage on Tuesday, 12 June 1934 caused a mild sensation. He arrived in the afternoon, toured the town, eschewed the theatre (he spoke no English) but walked to the Picture House and sat through the whole programme, hoping, it was said, to see his week's visit to Britain in the newsreels (but in vain). At the Shakespeare Hotel he gave numerous autographs, no mere scrawling of a name but a work of art. At 5 a.m. next morning he was rowed up the river and at 10.30 a.m. he left, to visit the church, the Birthplace and Anne Hathaway's Cottage, before going on to Warwick Castle.

55   Proclamation of Edward VIII

The news that 'the King's life is moving peacefully towards its close', broadcast on 22 January 1936, spread swiftly and people dispersed quietly to their homes to hear subsequent bulletins. Parties broke up, clubs and pubs were emptied and lighted windows gleamed through the winter night long after the usual hours of retirement as people kept their vigils waiting for news. Between announcements a metronome ticked in the silence. The end came just after midnight. As the Herald reported: 'One by one the lights in the windows went out; the watch was over.' Next morning the Mayor and the Corporation gathered at the Town Hall and from the steps proclaimed to the assembled crowd King Edward VIII. He was already a much loved royal figure whose visits to Stratford were warmly remembered, the most recent being less than four years previous. Stratford prepared to celebrate, after the official mourning for George V, the Coronation of his successor.

56 Proclamation of George VI

Less than a year passed when the unthinkable happened and the King of eleven months abdicated to marry the woman he loved. Again the Council was gathered. Sunday morning, 13 December the Mayor led the Corporation to Market Cross in procession from the Town Hall, to join the assembled Cadets, Legion, Scouts and Guides and a large number of borough officials and the public. Following the proclamation of George VI three cheers were raised for his Majesty, the National Anthem was sung and the procession moved off to the Holy Trinity, where the Vicar welcomed the Council to their accustomed places. Thanks to the Mayor (Councillor Ray) deciding to proclaim the new king on Sunday (in glorious sunshine), Stratford became the first place in England apart from the court of St. James and London to make the proclamation. Most other towns and cities waited until Monday and made their proclamations in rain and gales.

57 Coronation Pageant 12 May 1937

Stratford celebrated the Coronation of King George VI and Queen Elizabeth 'in a manner worthy of the town'. The success of the street pageant exceeded, said the Herald, the wildest hopes of the organizers. Stratford's well-known and often manifested propensity for dressing up and performing was fully exploited as clubs and businesses, industries and organizations, amateur and professional sportsmen and women, and all sorts and conditions of townsfolk joined in. The Grammar School had a tableau of the Gower Memorial on a horse-drawn dray, followed by boys representing rowing, cricket, rugby, boxing and the Cadet Corps. Festivities went on until long after dark, with illuminations and fireworks and parties everywhere.

58 Coronation party in Bordon Place

The Herald was full of Coronation reports, pages and special photographs of events. Street dinners were arranged everywhere as groups of streets feasted together under their local committee chairmen. 'A Right Royal Spread at Bordon-place' was one headline. 'Upwards of 90 children, attended by parents and friends enjoyed "a royal spread" on the centre piece of the municipal estate of Bordon-place.' The feast consisted of ham, lettuce and salmon sandwiches, trifle, fruit, cream and ices and lemonade and milk, Packets of sweets and newly-minted three-penny pieces were distributed to the children. The feast ended with cheers for their Majesties and the National Anthem. Scenes like this were repeated all over town and in every housing estate.

59 Bollands' new Garage and pumps

Bollands, the established cycle shop in Henley Street, expanded its business in 1937 to take advantage of the fast-growing motor trade. Stratfordians had been buying cars for years and the new extension of Bollands' premises from Henley Street through to Guild Street gave them showroom space for the extensive range of cars for which they acted as agents. It also allowed them to install the new electric petrol pumps at which Councillor Ray (the Mayor) filled his tank. This the pumps did 'in a remarkably brief time and visibly calculating the cost of the refill to the customers; a rather alarming process indicating only too clearly the cost of modern speed and progress'.

60   Planting of the Coronation Oak

The last page of the last issue of the Herald for 1937 noted that there was considerable disappointment in Stratford-on-Avon that the authorities did not mark Coronation year by planting suitable trees in appropriate places. It was left for the Trustees of Shakespeare's Birthplace to lead the way by planting trees on their land at Welcombe. Earlier in the autumn Sir G.M. Trevelyan, whose family had owned Welcombe, spoke of his regret that no taxpayers' money was spent preserving the beauty of nature and landscapes. 'Pictures and objets d'art, yes; but natural beauty, no.' The Herald urged that only by judicious planting of trees and more trees by the authorities and by private people can the beauty of our surroundings be assured.

61 Stratford Amateur Players

The Stratford Amateur Players were previously part of the Amateur Operatic and Dramatic Society, but by 1937 the two groups had gone their separate ways. The Players were not as financially successful as their Operatic Society colleagues, and were reduced to presenting their productions in the confined space of the Memorial Theatre lecture room. This meant producing small intimate works which suited the smaller space, and the players were commended by their reviewers for undertaking as well all the stage management and scene painting. Their first production of the 1937-1938 season was 'Art and Mrs. Bottle' by Benn Levy. In December they presented 'If Four Walls Told.' In the photograph taken in front of the Memorial Theatre a few Stratfordians may see still see their younger selves.

The Hippodrome in Wood Street started life as a skating rink behind 21-22 Wood Street. In 1912 it was converted and opened as the Stratford-upon Avon Hippodrome and Cinema Deluxe, equipped with modern tip-up seats, electric light and 'now the equal to any Hall in the Provinces'. Its uses over the years were many – variety theatre, cinema, 'palais de danse', bingo hall, roller-skating rink. It was used for whist drives, amateur dramatics, wrestling, cage bird shows, lectures, concerts, meetings, treasure hunts, raffles and carnivals. It was not a noticeable feature of Wood Street, its entrance being a double doorway between two premises, but it offered facilities no other premises in town could provide. The photograph shows the tables set for Mop Day lunch, 12 October 1938, with places set for several hundred. Redevelopment came in 1971. Nos. 21 and 22 expanded to fill in the entrance and the Hippodrome was no more.

63 Nazi flag in Bridge Street

23 April 1939 was the Diamond Jubilee of the Memorial Theatre opening, but organizing the Birthday Celebrations that year was exceptionally difficult because of the international situation. Since the middle of 1938 the Herald had been reporting and advising on the preparations for war. Trenches were being dug in Arden Street in September 1938, air raid precautions were being drawn up. There was uncertainty about flying flags of countries recently 'liquidated' and plans for diplomatic representatives were liable to revision right up to the last minute. But the Swastika, as well as the flag of the new Spanish regime both flew. Two 'untoward' incidents occurred following the firing of the maroon which released the Union Jack. The German Chargé d'Affaires pulled the wrong cord and brought his country's flag hurtling to the ground and the Japanese flag also refused to fly, so that the escort 'had to swing on the cord'.

At the annual cadet inspection on 25 July at King Edward Sixth School, the Corps carried arms for the first time. They impressed the inspecting officer Col. the Hon. Cyril Siddeley of the 7th Battalion of the Royal Warwickshire Regiment with their keenness and interest, their open and close order marching, signalling, first aid and physical training. Several of those cadets were soon to join the Territorial Army, becoming part of D Company of the Royal Warwickshire Regiment which drilled in the Grammar School quad. On 14 July Stratford had had a practice full black-out. Messrs. N.C. Joseph were building air raid shelters, and there was no doubt that war was coming. Among those cadets pictured here are many still in Stratford, as well as many who were lost in the war, including Cadet Company Sergeant-Major Richard Spender, a young and talented poet.

65 Auxiliary Fire Service

The Auxiliary Fire Service, in October 1939, with its sixty members, was being trained and equipped to function as part of the wartime National Fire Service. Its station was in Guild Street and the photograph shows Fireman Smith on the left with the AFS trailer pump and his crew. During the dreadful night of 14/15 November 1940 the Stratford men and equipment went to the aid of Coventry, which that night was pounded by nearly five hundred German aircraft, six hundred tons of high-explosives and thousands of incendiaries (to quote Churchill). The Stratford team, with its old vehicle, called by its crew 'the Flying Bedstead' spent the night in that devastation, lost its Flying Bedstead and returned next morning blackened and silent. Some of those men never recovered from that night. Through the whole of the war no bomb fell on Stratford nor did it suffer any enemy damage, though some bombs were apparently dumped in nearby fields as bombers returned to Germany.

66 The last tramway wagon

The tramway wagon which stands at the town centre end of the Tramway Bridge is the last remnant of an undertaking which, in the words of John Norris, in his book The Stratford & Moreton Tramway, 'gave 135 years of service to the district'. Traces of the roadway remain, between the stations of Shipston and Stratford and Moreton and the raised section in Stratford is one of the town's favourite walks. The Tramway carried freight and passengers and connected the district with the thriving commercial waterfront wharves at Stratford. The passenger service ceased in the summer of 1929 and the intermediate stations closed in 1941. The last freight train to Shipston was in May 1960 and demolition began the following year.

67 Warwickshire Home Guard's 4th Battalion

Anthony Eden's plan to raise what he called Local Defence Volunteers was proposed in the spring of 1940, following the evacuation of Dunkirk. But Churchill didn't like the name and changed it to Home Guard. Stratford men formed the A Platoon of the Warwickshire Home Guard. Stratford did not really consider itself a target but 'accidents will happen' and the ARP, the Chief Fire Officer and the Sub-Controller of Civil Defence were all urging vigilance, preparedness with buckets and sand for incendiary bombs and above all complete blackouts. At a 4th Battalion rifle meeting on 20 April 1941 the Stratford team won the team cup by 21 points. The Herald commented: 'It must give a feeling of security to the local residents to realize that, should an invasion take place or enemy parachute troops appear in the district, the deadly markmanship of the local force may be a means of putting up an effective defence.' The Home Guard had its farewell parade on 4 December 1944. No casualties were recorded in Stratford during the war.

68   Mayor receives his new ration book

Rationing was introduced in November 1939 for meat, butter and margerine, cooking fats, lard, dripping and sugar. In November 1941 previously unrationed foods such as canned goods and jam were allotted points which varied according to supplies. Everyone with a ration card was entitled to buy goods up to a total of 16 points, later raised to 20. The Mayor, Councillor John Knight, took his place in the queue. Ministry of Food Information boards were displayed in the Gas Showrooms at 27 Wood Street and the Electricity Showrooms in Henley Street. Weekly news bulletins on current food supplies and recipes issued by the Ministry of Food would appear on these boards and housewives were urged to visit these showrooms.

69   'This is Britain'

In 1942 the BBC scheduled a series of broadcasts for transmission in the Overseas Service to Africa and North America called 'This is Britain' and the first of this series was recorded in June in Shakespeare's Birthplace, and called 'A Visit to Stratford-upon-Avon'. It was arranged by Joan Littlewood of the BBC and John Bird and taking part were Kent Stevenson, a Canadian; Bill Horniblow, a 75 year old farmer; Mrs. Ashby from Home Farm in Whitchurch; Doris Southam, 18, of Flowers Brewery; Charlie Collins, 35 years a boatman on the Avon; and Sam Bennett, the fiddler from Ilmington whose 'stories and songs came over with a richness of dialect that will delight and puzzle the English-speaking world'. Margaretta Scott spoke for the theatre. The Herald concluded: 'As will be seen, the feature compressed a good deal into its 15 minutes. It should carry a fragrant message to listeners overseas who wish us well in our present struggle and have a specially warm place in their hearts for Shakespeare's home town.'

70 Princess Royal's Red Cross visit on 6 July 1944

King George VI's sister the Princess Royal was a tireless worker during the war, visiting hospitals and helping fund-raising events everywhere. One such was an exhibition, held in the Stratford Town Hall to raise money for the Duke of Gloucester's Red Cross Fund and the St. John Fund, and the Princess Royal came to Stratford to open the exhibition. In her official British Red Cross uniform she was cheered through the decorated streets of the town and welcomed at the Town Hall by Lady Helen Seymour, President of the Warwickshire branch, whom she congratu-lated for all the efforts of her branch. After the Town Hall she visited the Emergency Hospital and then the Shottery Hall Auxiliary Hospital, where her guard of honour (pictured here) was formed by the Hall nursing and domestic staff, Red Cross and St. John Cadets and children of St. Andrew's School, Shottery.

From the outbreak of war the Women's Land Army filled the gaps left when the farm workers went to war. Volunteers for this work were expected to be sporting and out-door women, but, said the Herald, for every riding instructor or games-mistress there were three or four housewives, shop assistants, office or factory workers. Adaptability and a willingness to learn were more important than brawn or toughness. After a little more than a year the Women's Land Army in Warwickshire had 210 members in full-time employment, and they were regarded by farmers as a source of really useful labour. That was the official view, but some farmers found, to begin with, that the new labour force was quite unprepared for the realities of life on the farm, and took some careful coaching in the finer points of tractor-driving, milking, thatch-making, silage-carting, animal husbandry and country living in all weathers. The dress uniform for the WLA was corduroy breeches, green jumpers, khaki hats and mackintoshes with badges and armlets. These six girls are off duty by the Bancroft Basin.

72 Victory Thanksgiving service

'Mood of Subdued Thankfulness Pervaded All' was the Herald headline describing Stratford's reaction to the news of 8 May 1945 that the war in Europe was over. 'The great occasion for which hearts had been hungering this many a year... liberty had triumphed (but at what a cost), freedom was victorious...' The following Sunday afternoon at a public service in Bridge Street, all denominations joined in thanksgiving – the Mayor. Councillor Roderick Baker, civic officials, the Vicar, the Salvation Army band, the choirs of all the churches, the Fire Service, the Home Guard 'splendidly alert as if they did not know what "stand down" meant'. And round and about, in the car park, on the footpath, at windows overlooking the street, throngs joined in. At the same time, in St. Paul's Cathedral, and in every city and town people gathered to give thanks and to remember what victory had cost.

73 Victory Street parties

VE-Day in May and VJ-Day in August were both followed by an explosion of street parties. 'Good neighbours are a blessing to themselves and to others. What a lot they can do when they co-operate.' The Herald reported in detail the Celebration street teas and dances and parties held all over town with neighbourhoods sharing the work and the expense. Shottery Road, West Street, Narrow Lane, Chestnut Walk, Shakespeare Street, Rother Street, Sanctus Road, Park Road, Elm Road, Ely Street – everywhere the neighbours enjoyed themselves abundantly. 'Well done Stratford!' concluded the Herald. The picture is of Wellesbourne Grove's children's party.

In the early hours of 5 December 1946 a disastrous fire destroyed the upper part of the Town Hall, and with it the famous Gainsborough portrait of David Garrick, painted for the Garrick Jubilee to mark the restoration of the Town Hall in 1769. The painting had only recently been restored to the Town Hall after being removed for safe-keeping during the war. (Ironically, Stratford suffered no damage during the war.) There was a dance at the Town Hall on 4 December which had ended at 1 a.m. and the custodian, Fred Baker, retired to bed shortly afterwards. He was awakened at 4.30 a.m. by a postal worker who had seen flames. Though efforts were made to reach the ballroom the smoke and flames were too intense and the Gainsbor-

ough and several other large pictures perished. The ground floor was saved by the concrete floor of the ballroom

above, but firemen and members of the gathering crowd helped to remove valuable furniture, regalia, silver and

pictures from the ground floor to nearby premises. The ballroom was re-opened two years later on 10 December.

75 Postcard from post-war Stratford

A 1940s visitor to Stratford returning fifty years later would have no trouble recognizing the town he saw then, though much of the surroundings have changed. From the five views of this postcard it is only necessary to remove or update the automobiles, and perhaps remove the street awnings, to find the town centre of old. There are more people, certainly, and it is sometimes impossible to walk on those pavements without encountering a tour guide with a crowd of followers. But the Shakespeare Hotel, Harvard House, the Guild Chapel and the Grammar School, with the Falcon Hotel in the foreground are as they were. The Shakespeare (Gower) Memorial holds its place but the Bankcroft Basin behind it is now never without several boats moored and visitors watching the canal traffic. The photograph of the Great Garden of New Place could have been taken any summer day of the intervening years.

76 Holy Trinity on the Avon

'Through all the changing scenes of life' to quote the old hymn, the parish church has watched over the town, and although removed from the geographical town centre it has nevertheless been the heart of the life of Stratford-upon-Avon, as the river beside which it stands has been its raison d'être. None of life's events were unmarked by the parish church and its Mayors, no matter what their personal denominations, led their Councils there at the beginning of the Mayoral year. Weddings, funerals, memorial services for Kings and commoners, times of peril and times of thanksgiving, weddings, christenings, and private griefs and joys were all there. No civic event was complete without the Vicar, who was also the Mayor's Chaplain. The River Avon, though visited by thousands, and fished and rowed as it has always been, can still be enjoyed in its tranquillity in all seasons. This scene is, and must always remain, timeless.

Holy Trinity Church, Stratford-upon-Avon.